The Great Songs of Chicago.

Wise Publications
London/New York/Sydney/Cologne

M 3449

4·50

Exclusive Distributors:
Music Sales Limited,
8/9 Frith Street, London W1V 5TZ, England.
Music Sales Pty. Limited,
120 Rothschild Avenue, Rosebery, NSW 2018, Australia.

This book © Copyright 1985 by
Wise Publications
ISBN 0.7119-0681-5
Order No. AM39702

Designed by Pearce Marchbank and Philip Levene
Cover photography by L.F.I.
Compiled by Peter Evans

Music Sales complete catalogue lists thousands of
titles and is free from your local music book shop,
or direct from Music Sales Limited.
Please send £1 in stamps for postage to
Music Sales Limited, 8/9 Frith Street, London W1V 5TZ.

Printed in England by:
JB Offset Printers (Marks Tey) Limited,
Marks Tey, Essex

The Great Songs of Chicago.

If You Leave Me Now.

Words & Music: Peter Cetera

don't go. / don't go. 2.) And if you Ooh,

girl, I just want you to stay.

A love like ours is love / We've come too far to leave

that's hard to find. / it all be-hind. How could we let / How could we end

it slip a-way?
it all this way?

When to-mor-row comes, then we'll both

re-gret the things we said to-day.

take a - way _ the big - gest part _ of me. _ Ooh, _

no, _____ ba - by, please _____ don't go.

Ooh, _____ girl, _____ I've got to have ____ you by ____ my side. _____
Sweet ma - ma, _____ just got to have ____ your love in-side ____ me. ____

Repeat and fade

Ooh, _____

8

Hard Habit To Break.

Words & Music: Stephen Kipner and John Lewis Parker

Hard To Say I'm Sorry.

Words & Music: Peter Cetera and D. Foster

hard for me to say I'm sor - ry, I just want you to stay.
hard for me to say I'm sor - ry, I just want you to know.

Aft - er all that we've been through, I will make it up to you, I pro -

- mise to, and aft - er all that's been said and done you're just

a part of me I can't let go.

Hold me now, I real - ly want to tell you I'm sor - ry.

Wishing You Were Here.

Words & Music: Peter Cetera

Oo,

Same old show in a dif - f'rent town on an - oth - er time. Oo,

Wish - ing you were here.
Wish - ing you were here.

Ev - en though you're far a - way, you're on my mind. Oo,

But, I've got my job to do, and I do it well,

So I guess that's how it is.

Oo, Wish-ing you were here. Oo, Wish-ing you were

here. Oo. Wish-ing you were here. Wish-ing you were here.

On the road, it's a heav-y load, but, I'll get by. Oo,

Wish-ing you __ were here. __
Wish-ing you __ were here. __

Pay the price; __ make a sac - ri - fice, __ and still I'll try. __ Oo, _____ Wish-ing you __ were

here, __
Wish-ing you __ were here. __ Oo, _____ Wish - ing you __ were

Oo. _____
here. _____
Wish-ing you __ were here.

Make Me Smile.

Words & Music: Peter Pankow

Make Me Smile. ____

Colour My World.

Words & Music: Peter Pankow

Questions 67 and 68.

Words & Music: Robert Lamm

25 or 6 to 4.

Words & Music: Robert Lamm

1. Wait - ing   for ___ the   break ___ of   day, ___
2. Star - ing   blind - ly   in - to   space, ___
3. Feel - ing   like ___ I   ought ___ to   sleep, ___

29

Saturday In The Park.

Words & Music: Robert Lamm

sto - ries his own way._____ Lis-ten chil-dren, all____ is not lost;___ all

___ is not lost,____ oh _____ no,___ no.

D. S. al Coda

Coda

Does Anybody Really Know What Time It Is?

Words & Music: Robert Lamm

I said,   "Does an - y - bod - y real - ly

know what time ____ it is; ____   Does an - y - bod - y real - ly   care?

If so, I can't ____ im - a - gine why   We've all got   time ____ e - nough to cry."

We've all got   time ____ e - nough to die."

Call On Me.

Words & Music: Lee Loughnane

Baby What A Big Surprise.

Words & Music: Peter Cetera

41

Alive Again.

Words & Music: James Pankow

Yes - ter - day I __ would not have be-lieved __ that __ to - mor - row __ the

sun would shine. Then __ one __ day you __ came in - to my life; __

I am a - live_____ a - gain.____ I am a - live_

___ a - gain. ___

All the emp - ty yes -
When you gave ___ your love ___

- ter - days ___ have dis - ap - peared, ___
___ to me ___ you changed my ___ life. ___

now that you ___ have filled ___ my life ___ with ___ love. _____
Dreams that once ___ seemed hope - less come ___ with ___ ease. _____

Don't you know I'm feel-in' a - live. _____

1. Solo ad lib _

2. (lead vocal) Yes - ter - day _____ that __ to - mor -
   (Background vocal)   I would not __ be-lieve _____   the

- row __ Then one day _____
sun was gon - na shine. __   you came in - to __ my life. _____

Repeat and Fade

I am a - live _____ a - gain. _____

The Great Songs of George Harrison.

ISBN 0.7119.0562.2
Order Np. AM37649

The Great Songs of Chris DeBurgh.

ISBN 0.7119.0464.2
Order No. AM35536

The Great Songs of Michael Jackson.

ISBN 0.7119.0483.9
Order No. AM36401

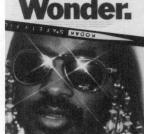

The Great Songs of Stevie Wonder.

ISBN 0.7119.0421.9
Order No. AM34596

The Great Songs of The Police.

ISBN 0.7119.0550.9
Order No. AM37565

The Great Songs of Al Stewart.

ISBN 0.7119.0666.1
Order No. AM39587

The Great Songs of John Denver.

ISBN 0.7119.0563.0
Order No. AM37656

The Great Songs of The Carpenters.

ISBN 0.7119.0638.6
Order No. AM39108

The Great Songs of Barry Manilow.

ISBN 0.7119.0561.4
Order No. AM37631

The Great Songs of Cat Stevens.

ISBN 0.7119.0564.9
Order No. AM37664

The Great Songs of The Rolling Stones.

ISBN 0.7119.0593.2
Order No. AM38225

The Great Songs of Rod Stewart.

ISBN 0.7119.0680.7
Order No. AM39694

The Great Songs of Chicago.

ISBN 0.7119.0681.5
Order No. AM39702

The Great Songs of Gordon Lightfoot.

ISBN 0.7119.0391.3
Order No. AM34109

The Great Songs of Chris DeBurgh.

ISBN 0.7119.0697.1
Order No. AM 39900

Great Songs, Great Series.

The greatest songs by the greatest
performers and songwriters of our times.
A handsomely presented, very collectable set of beautifully engraved music,
all in full piano/vocal arrangements with complete lyrics,
guitar chord boxes and symbols.
The most economical way of buying sheet music today.

Available from your local music dealer,
or contact . . .
Music Sales Limited,
8/9 Frith Street,
London W1V 5TZ.

6/89